Message to the Masses

Workbook

Julia A. Royston

BK
ROYSTON
Publishing

BK Royston Publishing
P. O. Box 4321
Jeffersonville, IN 47131
502-802-5385
http://bkroystonpublishing.com
bkroystonpublishing@gmail.com

© Copyright – 2015

Published by: BK Royston Publishing LLC

Cover Design: Bill Lacy Graphics

ISBN-13: 978-0692371695 (BK Royston Publishing)

ISBN-10: 0692371699

Printed in the United States of America

Other Titles by
Julia A. Royston

A New Season in Word: Inspirations for Divine Living - © 2007
How Hot is Your Love Life? Return to Your First Love - © 2008
Everyday Miracles-© 2010
Frontline Worshipper — © 2011
All New Season in Word — ©2012
30 Lessons the Student Taught the Teacher - ©2013
 The Gifted ©2014
Marianne the Librarian ©2014
Message to the Masses ©2014
Building the Dream Team ©2014
To Mom with Love, Mother's Day Anthology ©2014
The Miracle of Love at Christmas ©2014

Music by Julia A. Royston

Joy in His Presence – © 2004
Hymns for Him – © 2005
A New Season in Word and Song – © 2007
For Your Glory Lord—© 2009
Everyday Miracles—©2010
Frontline Worshipper - ©2011 - Published by juju 4ee Publishing

Acknowledgement

I thank my Lord and Savior Jesus Christ for giving me another opportunity to introduce more people to you. I thank you that you have entrusted this gift to me. Lord, let your Spirit move, guide and empower through this book to the people who will read it.

To my husband, Brian K. Royston, the love of my life for loving and cheering me on so much that I can be and do all that God has placed in me. I love you...

To my Mom, who is my greatest supporter and best friend. To my Dad, who is in heaven, that I know is proud of me and always encouraged me to go for it. Thanks to all of the rest of my family for their love and support.

A special thank you to Rev. and Mrs. Claude R. Royston for their love and support.

I dedicate this book to every person in the world. No matter the product, service, ministry, gift, talent, organization, business, small or great, let something that is written in this book help you to move closer to your goal of success and moving your Message to the Masses.

Love, Julia A. Royston

Dedication

I dedicate this to every person who has ever been told that you are local, no one will ever know about you and you will not succeed. Prove them wrong and go do it.

I pray that you get the courage to keep going, strength from God to keep growing and knowledge from the masters to keep knowing.

Introduction

The Message to the Masses book is designed to assist owners and operators of business, organizations, non-profits and ministries utilize social media and other tools to get their message to a broader audience. I have found that one of the main reasons that the message is not spread correctly is that company representatives don't know what the message is and can articulate it clearly.

The purpose of the Message to the Masses Workbook is to "write the vision and make it plain." There is something about putting your thoughts, goals and ideas on paper. Additionally, if an entire team is working on these thoughts, goals and ideas of the visionary, a clearer, focused and targeted vision should develop.

Take these tools and create the organization that will stand the test of time.

Julia A. Royston..

Table of Contents

Chapter 1

Purpose and Message

There is an intended use and purpose for everything that is created. There is always a message that your organization, business, ministry, products or services wants to deliver along with that purpose. Let's think about the purpose and message of your organization, business, ministry, products, services or your life.

In the space below, *Write the Purpose* of your organization, business, ministry, product or service?

_____

_____

_____

_____

_____

_____

_____

_____

_____

In the space below, write the message that your organization, business, ministry, products, services or life is striving to deliver.

_____

_____

_____

_____

_____

_____

_____

_____

_____

_____

_____

_____

Write a condensed version of that same message in 25 words or less.

Now write an even more condensed version of that same message in seven (7) words or less.

_____

_____

_____

_____

_____

Message Statement –In the space below, create a message or mission statement

about your business, organization, ministry, products, services or life.

_____

_____

_____

_____

_____

_____

Email Signature – Write a synopsis version of your message as it will appear in your signature portion on your email. (Note: there is very limited space in an email signature.) For example, the email signature for BK Royston Publishing LLC is "Treating You and Your Books Like Royalty"

_____

_____

_____

_____

_____

Hashtags - Determine several hashtag statements for your organization that relate to your organization, business, products, services or life. For example, I often use #messagetothemasses for this book, coaching call and live events. For example, #bkroystonpublishing

_____

_____

_____

_____

_____

_____

_____

_____

_____

Chapter 2
Products and Services

Now, that you know your purpose and the message of your purpose, what are the products and services that you are going to sell or offer that relate to your purpose and message?

Signature Products

_____

_____

_____

_____

_____

_____

_____

_____

_____

_____

Secondary Products

_____

_____

_____

_____

_____

_____

_____

_____

_____

_____

Trial or Temporary Products

_____

_____

_____

_____

_____

_____

_____

_____

_____

_____

Seasonal Products

_____

_____

_____

_____

_____

_____

_____

_____

_____

_____

What are some products or services that can evolve or develop as a result of your purpose and message?

For example, coaching, teleseminars, eBooks, television, video, movie, spoken word, stage play, radio or other social media outlet? Brainstorm some options below.

_____

_____

_____

_____

_____

_____

_____

_____

_____

_____

_____

_____

_____

_____

_____

_____

_____

_____

List the Services that you currently offer or would like to offer in the future.

_____

_____

_____

_____

_____

_____

_____

_____

_____

Rate your Customer Service

_____Excellent

_____Good

_____Fair

_____Poor

_____Needs Much Work

Based on how you rated your customer service, do you have any customer service needs? List them.

_____

_____

_____

_____

_____

_____

_____

_____

Goals

Goal setting is key to production, motivation and decision making. What are some goals that you have for your organization, business, products, services or life?

_____

_____

_____

_____

_____

_____

_____

_____

_____

_____

_____

_____

_____

_____

_____

_____

Sales Goals

_____

_____

_____

_____

_____

_____

_____

_____

_____

_____

_____

_____

_____

_____

_____

_____

_____

Staffing Goals

_____

_____

_____

_____

_____

_____

_____

_____

_____

_____

_____

_____

_____

_____

_____

_____

_____

_____

Operational Goals

_____
_____
_____
_____
_____
_____
_____
_____
_____
_____
_____
_____
_____
_____
_____
_____
_____

What are the actions steps and projected due dates to reach some of the goals listed?

Goal	Action Steps	Due Date

What is in your current inventory or collection of resources that will help you reach your business goal?

_____

_____

_____

_____

_____

_____

_____

_____

_____

_____

_____

_____

_____

What do you need to actually realize your goal?

_____

_____

_____

_____

_____

_____

_____

_____

_____

_____

_____

_____

_____

_____

_____

_____

_____

Evaluate the Goal Setting Process. Now, that you are working on your goal, what things didn't you consider that you should have *before* you began working on your goal?

_____

_____

_____

_____

_____

_____

_____

_____

_____

_____

_____

_____

_____

_____

_____

Chapter 3
Payments and Processes

Now that you have a purpose and offering products and services, how will people pay you for these services? Be sure to consider local, regional and international customers when they wish to pay you for services. Technology has made it possible and easier than ever before to transact business globally.

What are some payment options that you currently have in place for your organization, business or ministry?

_____Cash

_____Checks

_____Credit Cards

_____PayPal

_____Cash.me

_____Squareup.com

_____Merchant Account

_____Electronic Transfers

_____Mobile Credit Card Swiper Devices that can be attached to phone or other mobile device

Processes

What processes do you have in place to deliver your goods, products and services to your clients, customers or business partners?

_____Local postal mail delivery

_____Express mail delivery

_____Digital download of audio and video products from website

_____Digital download of audio and video products from 3rd party website

_____Audio and Video software for tele summits, webinars and teleconferences

_____Conference calling service for teleconferences and tele summits

_____Warehouse delivery for direct ordering and mail service to your clients

_____Personal inventory of products and services and delivery personally to customers

_____Virtual assistant handles orders

_____Automated process for email marketing and list building

_____My products and services are actually stored and displayed in a brick and mortar building

_____My products and services are virtual or when I appear at live shows and events.

For help with set-up or additional information for any of these processes, reach out to Julia Royston Enterprises at roystonjulia@gmail.com or call 502-802-5385.

Processes Assessment

Now that you have seen a list of possible processes for delivery of your products and services, what process do you need to better serve your customers? List them here.

_____

_____

_____

_____

_____

_____

_____

_____

_____

_____

_____

_____

_____

_____

_____

_____

_____

Chapter 4

Profiles of the Team

To accomplish any major task, it takes a team. You can accomplish little on your own. You are limited as one person to manage a very large operation. In the end you will be burnt out. You need a team. You must establish early on in your business, organization or ministry some people that you trust to walk this process out with you. You can't be everywhere at the same but you must be careful who you put in place. If you are confident in your team, you need to provide a profile of your team members, their role and their contact information for your customer.

Who is all on your team? List them below

_____

_____

_____

_____

_____

_____

_____

_____

_____

_____

_____

_____

_____

_____

_____

_____

List your team member's name, role, and contact information below:

Name	Role	Contact Information

Biographical Sketch

Below is a basic framework for developing a biographical sketch. You can have your team complete this form for a biographical sketch. It can be condensed for your website, social media or any other outreach or promotional materials distributed concerning your business, organization, ministry or non-profit.

Name

_____

_____

City and State of Birth

_____

_____

Brief Family History

_____

_____

_____

_____

_____

_____

_____

_____

_____

_____

Educational Achievements

Awards, Professional Associations and Honors

Hobbies.

_____

_____

_____

_____

_____

_____

_____

_____

_____

_____

_____

_____

_____

_____

_____

_____

_____

Other Special Accomplishments

_____

_____

_____

_____

_____

_____

_____

_____

_____

_____

_____

_____

_____

_____

_____

_____

_____

_____

_____

_____

Chapter 5

People for the Message

Create a profile of the people that your message is intended to attract. Who is your audience? Is your audience primarily male or female? What do they eat, drink, drive, live in or hang out?

_____

_____

_____

_____

_____

_____

_____

_____

_____

_____

_____

Are there any groups of people that would be interested in your message, products or services? List them below:

_____

_____

_____

_____

_____

_____

_____

_____

_____

_____

_____

_____

The people and/or groups that you listed earlier, where do they hang out? Furthermore, are they still using email, the daily newspaper, and television news, Twitter, Facebook, Instagram or Pinterest to gain information or ideas for new purchases?

_____

_____

_____

_____

_____

_____

_____

_____

Chapter 6
Promotion and Marketing

Where do the people that you are targeting get their information?

_____

_____

_____

_____

_____

_____

_____

_____

_____

_____

_____

How will you deliver that message or what delivery method will you use? List the various ways of message delivery.

_____

_____

_____

_____

_____

_____

_____

_____

What is the best day and time of day to deliver that message to YOUR audience?

_____

_____

_____

_____

Chapter 7
Platform

Every time you speak about your business, promote your business, conduct your business, you are building a platform and wider audience to be attracted and connect with your business. Therefore, the more you talk about it, the further reach and the higher you are building the platform. A platform is a stand, position or representation of a specific industry or issue that you, your business or organization and message has taken upon itself.

If someone asked you about your foundational truths or platform that you have built your business, organization, ministry or non-profit on, what would that be?

_____

_____

_____

_____

_____

_____

_____

_____

_____

_____

_____

If you have a slogan, phrase or quote that you repeat about your business, what would that be?

_____

_____

_____

_____

_____

_____

_____

_____

_____

_____

Chapter 8

Partnerships and Collaboration

When getting your message to the masses you need as many references, helpers, word of mouth advertisers and references for using your business as possible. With all the technology that is available, recommendations and word of mouth is still the best promotional tool for your message.

List below at least ten people that with whom you could possibly partner.

_____

_____

_____

_____

_____

_____

_____

_____

_____

_____

_____

_____

_____

_____

_____

_____

_____

_____

_____

_____

List ten companies or industries that you can connect with and partner with in a venture. For example, my coaching company, Julia Royston Enterprises, LLC could partner with a community development company to provide training. Second example, my book publishing company could partner with a Youth Organization to inspire writing for spoken word, songs, etc.

_____

_____

_____

_____

_____

_____

_____

_____

_____

_____

_____

_____

_____

_____

_____

_____

_____

_____

_____

_____

Chapter 9
Pause to Grow

A business that is not changing, evolving, improving or being evaluated will soon die. Now that you are getting your message out to the masses how will improve your organization, business, product or service?

What workshops, conferences or retreats do sponsor for your team to attend?

_____

_____

_____

_____

_____

_____

_____

_____

_____

_____

_____

_____

What inside retreats, workshops or conferences do you host to allow your team to regroup, retreat and recover?

_____

_____

_____

_____

_____

_____

_____

_____

_____

_____

_____

_____

_____

Reflection Journal

Reflect on the things that went well, need for improvement and openly vent your feelings over the past 3 months, 6 months or year regarding your business, organization, ministry or non-profit.

_____

_____

_____

_____

_____

_____

_____

_____

_____

_____

_____

_____

Did your organization reach your goals or not? If not, why? If so, how and why?

_____
_____
_____
_____
_____
_____
_____
_____
_____
_____
_____
_____
_____
_____
_____
_____
_____

Moving Forward Journal

What to do differently 'moving forward?'

_____

_____

_____

_____

_____

_____

_____

_____

_____

_____

_____

_____

_____

_____

_____

_____

_____

_____

_____

NOTES

9 780692 371695